# Face the Fear

## Overcoming Public Speaking Anxiety

Dr. Todd Thomas

2nd Edition

For more information about this author visit
www.ImpactSuccess.com

ISBN 978-0-6151-7886-8

© 2006 Impact Publications   All rights reserved. No reproduction allowed except by express written consent of the publisher.

# Table of Contents

| | |
|---|---|
| Introduction | 3 |
| Chapter 1: The Public Speaking Experience | 7 |
| Chapter 2: Mind and Body | 19 |
| Chapter 3: What We Know and Think We Know | 31 |
| Chapter 4: Nervous Excitement vs. Nervous Anxiety | 41 |
| Chapter 5: Presenting the Speech | 59 |
| Chapter 6: The Final Word | 77 |

# Introduction

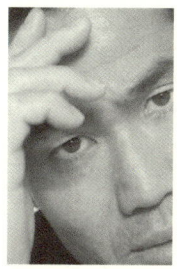

*My greatest weakness is the fear to speak in front of people. In one case, I made an excuse that I had a dentist appointment just so I wouldn't have to speak in front of the people where I work. Another thing that bothers me about speaking in front of people is that I'm afraid that I will make a fool out of myself or that I look stupid or sound stupid. What I want is to be able to walk up in front of a crowd and feel comfortable enough that my voice doesn't crack and I can give a smooth presentation without being scared to death.*

*I have never been able to get up in front of people without being scared to death. I had a speech class in high school and it was a very bad experience. I was extremely nervous with every speech I gave. I would tremble and shake; I even felt faint and very hot. My voice tends to be soft when I talk and then I talk very fast. As a speaker right now, I think I am horrible.*

Do these stories sound disquietingly familiar to you? Would you rather endure going to the dentist than give a public speech? Do memories of public speaking during your years in school continue to haunt you even as a working adult?

If so, you might be one of the tens of thousands of people who experience public speaking anxiety. There is no need to feel embarrassed or ashamed if you are afraid to speak in public. In fact, it is quite normal to be anxious in such situations. A famous Sunday Times research study of 3000 people in found that 41% reported fear of speaking in front of others as their number one anxiety before even death.

As many as 20 percent of people identify this anxiety as being severe. For some, a small case of nervousness makes the experience of public speaking a bit uncomfortable. For others, even the slightest idea of speaking in public is terrifying. No matter where you fall within this spectrum, together, we can formulate strategies to help you cope, succeed, and excel in your public presentations.

It is crucial to create a plan of attack when you are preparing to speak in public. Attack is actually the correct word to use here because to achieve startling success as a public speaker, you must work diligently to overcome the obstacles that are placed in front of you. But as you will learn while reading this book, it is the roadblocks that you create for yourself which are often the most difficult to conquer. Together, we will succeed in defeating all of the issues that are preventing you from becoming the best presenter you can be.

One difficulty that you are likely to encounter at the prospect of giving a public presentation is an intense swirling of emotion within. This could be a good thing if you are one of those people who find that these intense emotions add to the excitement of the situation. The members of your audience will learn from and enjoy the sense of excitement that you will portray.

On the other hand, you may feel that your anxiety about giving a public speech is overwhelming and maybe even totally debilitating. If this describes your feelings, then you can learn to transform your own fears of being at the center of attention into a tool in your presenter's arsenal.

It might also be that your view on public speaking falls somewhere between these extremes. If you are one of these, you most likely find that your anxiety about public speaking interferes with your ability to enjoy the experience of giving a speech. But in contrast to the person who is literally immobilized at the thought of speaking in front of a group of people, you are able to give your presentation without shutting down.

For the majority who are able to give a presentation if necessary, the experience is not only uncomfortable but is normally not as effective as it could be due to the distraction of anxiety. Using this text as a guide, you will discover how to focus on your strengths as a communicator to compensate for the areas of challenge that are created through fear.

Your own enjoyment is one aspect of giving a public presentation that you likely neglect without even realizing it. While it is certainly true that your audience should be entertained and impacted by your presentation, it is also important for you to have a positive experience for yourself. In addition to having fun in the spotlight during a public appearance, learning from your colleagues at this sort of event is often very rewarding in-and-of itself. But it is a difficult to be truly open to such pleasures when you are jittery or afraid before, during, or after speaking in public.

This book is designed to help you examine your anxiety about public speaking and develop strategies for coping with this anxiety. As you read this book you will find that the problems associated with public speaking are not as unique to you as you might think. It is important to understand the genesis of this anxiety in yourself before creating a strategy to address the fear.

You will also find that there are methods and processes that you can use immediately to have an impact on your experience. Once you have established a strategy, and successfully implemented it, you will find your audiences to be more satisfied and your communication more effective.

# Chapter One

## The Public Speaking Experience

One of the key elements of a strategy to deal with anxiety about public speaking is to understand the common process that we all go through when faced with the possibility of giving a presentation. For some, this process leads to an enjoyable and successful experience, while for others the process is painful and laborious.

Whether enjoyable or not, the public speaking experience usually starts long before the public speaking event takes place. It may seem an impossible contradiction that something can start before it begins. But as you will read in the following pages, public speaking works in just such a way. In fact, by the time you have finished reading this book, you will probably wonder how anyone could ever miss such an obvious truth.

Most of us do not even think about public speaking until we find ourselves faced with the possibility that we are going to give a speech. The word "possibility" is emphasized because our public speech needn't be imminent for us to get anxious. If we think that there is even a remote chance we may have to give a speech, the feelings of dread can begin. And this is where you must begin your process of self-awareness.

For many people, the prospect of having to give a public presentation is uncomfortable. For others, the mere thought of giving a speech to a group of people is enough to bring on symptoms of anxiety such as sleeplessness and physical discomfort. Katie describes her experience:

*I start getting nervous weeks before [the speech]. The same thing always happens. My stomach knots up and hurts like I have an ulcer or something. I go through nights where I can't get to sleep. Then there will be days when I can't stay awake. I remember when I first interviewed for this job and the personnel manager asked me if I had ever given a speech. I told him that I had, but inside I could feel my stomach knotting up again. Stupid, huh? He didn't ask me to give a speech, he just asked me if I ever had!*

It is obvious from Katie's story that our memories have a powerful influence over our behavior patterns. As children, we may have touched a hot stove in an attempt to figure out why it was glowing red and sending out heat. As adults, we know not to touch a hot stove because it has the potential to injure us and cause us physical pain. In other words, we learned from the otherwise negative experience of burning ourselves not to touch a stove while it is on. Likewise, many of us have discovered from first-hand experience and/or observation of others that public speaking is an unpleasant activity. Unfortunately, we are often tempted to have the same reaction to public speaking as we do to a hot stove – to never touch it.

Clearly, we already have the foundation for our public speaking experience: our assumptions about the nature of public speaking in general. We will discuss these assumptions in detail later, but for now we can divide them into two distinct schools of thought. The first is the Piece-of-Cake philosophy. The speaker who has these assumptions about public speaking sees no challenge in giving a presentation to a group of people. If there is a lot riding on the outcome of the speech, this speaker may be slightly nervous, but not too much.

The Piece-of-Cake speaker feels that making a speech is not difficult at all. All you have to do is undertake a little bit of research, make a few notes, pick out some nice clothing, and show up to give the speech. Nothing to it. This presenter sounds like he or she would be perfect for speaking in public. In reality, this speaker is likely overconfident in his or her own abilities. This can lead to a failure just as large as any other presenter might encounter. In the following pages, you will discover that there is a delicate balance between self-confidence and overconfidence.

The second school of thought is the Eating-Glass philosophy. Sounds painful doesn't it! For this speaker, there is absolutely, positively, no way on earth that the speech can be a success. This speaker feels that the only people who give good speeches are other people. This speaker also believes that if he or she had wanted to be an actor, then he or she would have gone to acting school. The idea of performing in front of a group, strangers or friends, is horrifying.

The Eating-Glass speaker often is not the least bit worried about the research part of the project. However, it does not matter how exciting or compelling the material turns out to be, this speaker is convinced that a bored audience will be the outcome. A presenter who tempers his or her own ego is on a path to success. However, a public speaker who convinces himself of herself that failure is inevitable will almost always find a way to make failure happen.

Both these types of speakers, Cake and Glass, may be erroneous in their assumptions. Cake is probably going to discover that the public speaking event requires a lot more thought and a lot more planning and preparation than he or she thinks at this point. Glass, on the other hand, would be relieved to discover that the actual public speaking event is rarely as bad as he or she thinks it is going to be.

Either way, these assumptions will immediately form the assessment of our personal ability when we discover that we may be chosen (or may have the opportunity) to give a public speech. You can see now how this can be a problem, especially if you tend to have the assumptions that our speaker Glass had earlier. If you assume that the public speaking event is a performance, then you immediately begin putting a lot of pressure on ourselves to "perform." You begin to think of yourself more as actors, and focus on the fact that there will be many pairs of eyes staring straight at you as you stand in front of them, trying your best to be a great orator.

As you assess your abilities, you imagine the lights and the focus of attention. You think about the "What would happen if I ... " scenarios and start imagining possible problems that could occur during our speech. By doing this, if you are like Glass, you will find that your self-assessment comes quite short of what you think a speaker's abilities should be to give a successful public presentation.

Once you have made your initial self-assessment based on your assumptions about public speaking, you then decide if you are truly capable of giving a good public speech. The answer to this question guides the outcome of your experience. If you decide that you are indeed capable of giving a successful presentation, then the nervousness you feel next will probably be best categorized as excitement. If you decide that you do not have the ability to give a good speech, then your nervousness becomes anxiety. As you continue to read, keep in mind that excitement and anxiety are not as different as they appear to be at first glance.

It is important to remember that your self-assessment is rarely, if ever, totally accurate. In fact, considering that you have not even begun putting together the speech yet, your self-assessment is based on the assumptions you have about your ability to do a speech. And your understanding of your ability to do the speech is based on the assumptions you have about public speaking. You may already be far removed from the reality of the situation through all of these assumptions.

Removing yourself from the reality of a presentation also removes you from the reality in which your audience will exist, and no doubt the reality in which your audience expects you to be. Maintaining a connection with your audience is imperative. If your audience is disconnected for your speech, you in fact have no audience at all.

If your assumptions lead you to the possible belief that you can indeed give a public speech successfully, then the resulting excitement will probably lead you into an active, motivated preparation of your speech. If you had a public speaking class earlier in life, you might try to find the old textbook or materials you used. You might go to the bookstore and see what books are available on the subject of writing a speech. The excitement that is involved in public speaking can lead you to interesting time spent in the library or on the Internet reading up on the topic, or perhaps to a few hours talking with experts or other relevant individuals on the subject.

On the other hand, if you doubt your ability to do well, then the anxiety related to public speaking can lead to near lethargy. You may find that you are unable to get started on the speech because you greatly dread the time when you are going to step in front of the audience.

These examples of excitement and lethargy can ignite a phenomenon known as the self-fulfilling prophecy. Sometimes, you get so caught up in your beliefs about a certain situation, that you actually create the outcome you expect to happen.

Indeed, avoidance becomes a key coping mechanism for many people when they are faced with speaking in public. Avoiding public speaking might mean avoiding the situation altogether, putting themselves in a position never to have to consider giving a presentation.

For those like Monica, avoidance of public speaking can take extreme proportions with harsh and very real consequences:

*I worked for a health agency and had tried for a long time to get the opportunity to make a sales presentation to a local bank. After several weeks of making phone contact, I finally was able to schedule the presentation. Although I've never been comfortable speaking to a group of people, I thought that this would be different since I had so much to gain from the experience. However, as the day grew closer I became more and more nervous. On the day of the presentation, I went into the conference room to set up my overhead and flip chart equipment. As everybody came into the room, the feeling of panic became almost overwhelming. Just before the chairman was going to introduce me, I told him I needed to step to the ladies' room for a minute. I walked out of the conference room, out of the bank, got into my car and went home. I never went back to the bank and, in fact, never went back to that health agency.*

Avoiding a horrendous outcome such as this is exactly what you will know how to do once you have completed this book. Being able to successfully complete a public appearance, help your employer, and enhance your professional reputation are much more desirable results that what happened to Monica.

For others who are unable or unwilling to run away, eventually giving a speech is inevitable. For these people, avoidance takes on a different appearance. These people put off preparing for the speech. Procrastination develops from their fear of doing a poor job. This procrastination can begin before you even start formulating your speech, leaving little time to actually get your thoughts together. In addition, since the thing most people dread most is the performance of the speech, procrastination can lead to a host of excuses that keeps you from practicing your speech ahead of time. Kerry's reaction is typical:

*When I find out I have to give a presentation, I initially want for myself to do well. But in the back of my mind, I contradict that and know I will do poorly. If think to myself, "I can't speak in front of these people. These people will think I am boring. They won't like what I am speaking about, etc." As a result, I usually can't bring myself to even start working on the speech until there is finally no choice.*

This passive preparation and procrastination will often lead to the very thing you fear the most — an unsuccessful public speaking event. Actually, for most people who experience public speaking anxiety, even a successful public speaking event can feel like an unsuccessful one. On the day or night of the event, you will discover that not only are you fearful of making a fool of yourself, but you are not as prepared as you should be and have thus increased the odds that your experience will be an awkward one. Then, regardless of whether or not the audience was pleased with the speech, you will give yourself a post speech negative assessment. This negative assessment is then filed in your brain for future public speaking opportunities.

If, on the other hand, you have convinced yourself that you are capable of giving a good speech, then you are more likely to have spent time preparing your speech, practicing your presentation, and focusing on making your audience understand your information or point of view. You will have increased the odds of having a positive public speaking experience and, as a result, give yourself a post-speech positive assessment. This positive assessment goes in the same "file drawer" in your brain as the negative assessment mentioned earlier, except that now the positive assessment will serve to encourage you the next time you face a public speaking event.

You are the one with the most power to control your own public speaking outcome. If you convince yourself before the fact that you are a poor public speaker, then you will almost surely remain closed to the possibility that you are capable of giving an informative and entertaining presentation. This can lead to giving a bad speech, or to a false sense of failure after a successful presentation. By allowing yourself to get enthusiastic about public speaking, you increase the chances that your speaking engagement will be a success. However, the likelihood that you will arrogantly assume an easy victory in the spotlight also goes up when your enthusiasm is given free reign.

The good news here is that these two ways of approaching a public speech are actually not so far removed from one another. Imagine that there are two hallways leading from the assessment of your personal ability to the final outcome assessment after the speech. Imagine there are several doors that connect the hallways as well. For example, you can learn to turn your anxiety into excitement and, by so doing, go through the door into the hallway leading to a successful public speaking event. You can also learn how to change your passive preparation and procrastination into a more active and effective preparation for your speech. By doing this, you will allow yourself to open the door into the hallway leading to success, positive self-assessment, and as a result, more success in the future.

Of course, all of this is easy to say. The real trick is to be able to put your mind and body into action. You may be tempted to give up and say, "I can't do it." But you have already taken the first step by purchasing this book. Perhaps you have a speech coming up soon and want to work on the experience now. Or maybe you've just finished a speech and want a better experience next time. The next step is to identify what your mind and body actually do at the awareness stage of the public speaking experience. As you will see in the next chapter, the mind and body do a lot!

# Chapter Two

## Mind and Body

When you become aware that you may have to give a speech, you begin a process within yourself that can be quite complex. By understanding how your psychological and physiological systems work together to help or hinder you, you well find yourself better able to control your own public speaking experience.

These systems operate almost identically for everybody. They are part of the human condition, that which binds all men and women together as a species. What is it then that makes some good at giving public speeches, while others encounter so many difficulties? It is the perception of your experiences that differ dramatically from person to person.

Milton and Annette offer interesting perceptions on the prospect of giving a public speech. Milton describes his public speaking experience as follows:

*One of the worst classes in my academic experience was my freshman public speaking class. I tried everything I could think of to get out of having to take the class. But for somebody interested in the business field, it was a requirement. I've seen a lot of good speakers out there, people who could stand up in front of fifty or five hundred people and talk as if they were talking to their best friends. I also knew that I wasn't one of these people. I think that I started getting nervous about my first speech around the day I bought the textbook for the class! I mean, my heart started racing, my mouth got dry, and my hands started sweating right there in the bookstore! Martin Luther King, Jr. I'm not. And I just knew I would make a fool out of myself.*

Annette described the same experience a different way:

*When I found out during the interview that my job would require my making informative presentations to outside interest groups, I knew this was the job for me. I remember the second interview for my current position, when you started talking about these speeches. I've always loved being on "center stage" and this seemed like just the thing. I recall I started getting excited right then, in the interview. I could hardly sit still, because I knew that this was the element of my new job that would make me successful. In fact, just thinking about that interview makes me remember the adrenaline rush I got when I imagined myself standing in front of these people, all their eyes turned to me, and me with their full attention.*

Wow! Who is this Annette person anyway? Do people really feel like that about public speaking? Is she for real? Well, yes. There are some people that go out of their way to find situations that will allow them to give public speeches. Not many, but a few... What's really interesting is to notice that Milton and Annette both describe the same physical responses to the same situation. Both of these people developed similar symptoms. Milton and Annette became very active. They were unable to remain calm or be still. They felt like moving and their bodies definitely reacted to having to remain civilized. However, one gets the sense that Milton wanted to go running out of the bookstore, to save himself by hiding from something unspeakably horrible. Annette wanted to go running up to the lectern so that she could be at the center of attention. What differentiates Annette's excitement from Milton's terror?

Your bodies are designed to react to strange or threatening situations in such a way as to allow a large range of options and possible responses. Long ago, it was important for us as humans to develop an instinct that would protect us from danger. This instinct in the face of physical threat, commonly called the fight or flight response, became a characteristic of early humans that aided the species in overcoming many evolutionary challenges. If Jane and Joe Cavepeople had not learned that certain creatures (the occasional woolly mammoth or, perhaps, other cave people) posed a threat to their existence, and had they not developed an instinctive ability to detect and react to this threat, then, as one scholar has put it, we would all be descended from a long line of extinct ancestors!

The problem with this fight or flight response is that you have not only learned it well; you have learned it too well. Remember the discussion about touching the burning-hot stove? A child who removes his hand from a hot surface the moment he begins to feel pain is experiencing a proper fight or flight response. In this example the child chooses flight, and correctly so. It wouldn't make much sense to try and fight the stove.

These instincts are correct when they serve a useful purpose by avoiding a negative consequence of some sort. Indeed, you face still more physical dangers in everyday life. Walking across the street and realizing that a car is speeding in your direction may require an immediate, instinctive response. Hopefully, in this case you will choose the flight option, since fighting an oncoming vehicle may not lead to a desired outcome. There are other times when your level of stress may be so great — such as when you think about standing in front of a group of people and delivering a speech — that you essentially mislead your body into thinking that you are in physical danger, that the fight or flight response is appropriate, when actually it is not.

You can measure this appropriateness in terms of consequences. Avoiding physical contact with a hot stove or scurrying out of the path of a speeding car will more than likely prevent you from being harmed. On the other hand, remember Monica. She most definitely had an extraordinary flight response – she lied to avoid a presentation that she had worked tirelessly to arrange, and even quit her job in a sense of embarrassment, guilt, and humiliation.

It is rare that a public speaking situation will put you at physical risk. Of course it is possible, but it is highly unlikely. It is even more unlikely that your audience is actually going to charge the podium when you make your presentation. You know that. Your audience knows that. And you know that your audience knows that.

Even so, if your level of anxiety about giving a speech is high, you may still experience many of the effects of the fight or flight response when you face your audience. Making a choice to stand your ground and confront (or fight) your fear may very well be one of the most difficult tasks that you will ever attempt to accomplish. But think of the alternatives for a moment: not graduating from college because of a failed public speaking class, losing your job, or worst of all having to live with a sense of personal failure.

A little later in this book, you will learn some strategies to help you confront your fears and boost your level of self-confidence. First, see if some of these reactions are familiar to you.

**Physiological Reactions**

When an individual faces a stressful situation, such as public speaking, the body passes along the stress signal to the hypothalamus and thalamus in the brain. When the hypothalamus receives this signal, it in turn activates two of your body's fight or flight systems: the autonomic nervous system and the endocrine system.

The autonomic nervous system then activates several other subsystems in your body. Involuntary body functions such as heart rate, breathing, and blood pressure are affected. Usual results are increased heart rate, higher blood pressure, and increased rate and depth of breathing. Further, the pituitary gland orders the release of aldosterone, which increases blood pressure; cortisol, which increases blood sugar and energy; epinephrine (adrenaline), which increases energy and releases several other stimulating chemicals into the body. As a result, you may experience physical anxiety, flushing of the skin, tremors in your voice, a decrease in body temperature, dryness of the mouth, or a quivering in various extremities.

Not everybody has the exact same reaction, but most people will experience at least one or two of these symptoms when faced with a high stressor such as public speaking. Colloquialisms like "butterflies in my stomach," "my heart is pounding," and "I'm a nervous wreck," are all ways of describing the physical manifestations of the autonomic nervous and endocrine systems as they react without your will to the experience of a public speaking situation.

**Behavioral Reactions**

As mentioned before, the most common, and most problematic, behavioral reaction to the public speaking event is to simply attempt to avoid it. Avoidance is common and can be achieved by simply not accepting the invitation or request to speak. Beside the consequence of missed opportunities, the social, job and peer pressures sometimes make total avoidance unrealistic. It is not only more beneficial, but more realistic to learn the skills needed to be an effective public speaker.

The next most common avoidance reaction is to make excuses and rationalizations. You attempt to do this through finding reasons for not giving the presentation. These reasons are as varied as the possible speaking situations, but can include such statements as "I'm not the right person for this speech," or "I really don't have time to do the research for a good presentation," or "You know, I'll try to get out of that dentist appointment on that day, but I'm not really sure that I can."

If you can't totally avoid the situation or excuse yourself from it without risking your career, you are left with what is probably the most uncomfortable yet common avoidance reaction: procrastination. If the excuses you make with others do not succeed in relieving you of the responsibility for giving the speech, then the excuses you use with yourself will at least put off the inevitable.

Unfortunately, procrastination also creates a spiral that can be self-defeating. By putting off the preparation for your presentation, you also keep yourself from having the time necessary to do a good job. Putting together a speech requires preparation. As you begin the research or as you sit down to construct an outline, you soon realize that you are committing yourself to something that you really feel uncomfortable doing. As a result, you wait as long as possible to do the necessary preparation and you create your self-fulfilling prophecy. In other words, you have a sense of foreboding that says you aren't going to do a good job on this public speech. Then, through procrastination, you guarantee it. Without proper preparation and practice, even the best public speaker is destined to fail.

You have then proven the point you set out to state at the beginning: You can't give a public speech. At the least, you feel you have proven the point when you don't do as well as you could have. Of course, the real reason in this case is that you didn't prepare properly. It will serve as another uncomfortable situation which will make you avoid the next public speaking situation even more. Now not only do you feel as if you can't stand up in front of people to make a presentation, you have at least one experience you can recall where you did give a presentation – and you did a poor job of public speaking.

In addition, somewhere deep down you know that the reason you didn't do well is because you didn't work at it, which adds to your sense of failure: failure to others, failure to your audience, and failure to yourself. While failing your audience and others, such as your employers or teachers, could certainly have negative consequences for your work or academic standings, failing yourself is perhaps the most damaging in the long term. If you fail yourself, then not only are you receiving criticism from the outside world, you are also being chastised from within. Being too critical of yourself is often damaging to your mental health as well as to your ability to speak well in public.

**Psychological Reactions**

The feeling of failure associated with avoidance actually can, and frequently does, appear before you've even given your presentation. First, there is the "I'm going to fail" period where you may find yourself setting expectations that are beyond realistic. You may spend hours designing the "perfect" visual aid. Or you may spend days on the Internet or make trip after trip to the library to find just one more piece of research or to read one more relevant argument, convincing yourself the whole time that you are going to do a poor job or "look stupid."

In moderation, this attention to detail can be quite helpful when it comes time to present a topic and answer questions from an audience. Taken to an extreme however, nitpicking can distract you from achieving all of your goals before a speech, the end result being that you are unprepared to face your audience. Indeed, you may even use a quest for perfection as a method of procrastination, again resulting in being under-prepared.

During the speech, many find that they are hyper-aware of the physiological reactions to stress they are experiencing. You may perceive that the slight leg shakiness you are feeling looks to the audience as if you are doing an Elvis impersonation. The red blotches you can see on your neck in a mirror appear to the audience as an atlas representation of the world's continents. Worrying too much about the physiological responses can make you lose your focus and concentration. Of course, you need focus and concentration most in difficult situations like speaking to a room filled with people!

Cognitive disruption... this is a rather academic-sounding term for what most of us would call a difficulty in keeping concentration. As just mentioned, there's the hyper-focus on yourself. You must also remember that the body has geared up in a way that gives you a lot excess energy, often too much for your own good. Your minds tend to wander, especially if you haven't prepared enough for the speech to begin with. You can find yourself easily distracted or forgetting an idea in mid-thought.

Then of course there's the post-speech period. You are likely your own worst critic. It is easy to feel that you have done a much less satisfactory job than most of your audience will feel you have done. Your perception of your performance is clouded by your own self-doubts. A speech that to the audience seemed perfectly fine can seem to you like an abysmal failure. Unfortunately, if you are hypercritical, you don't often weigh the evidence for or against your performance. Rather, you depend on your feelings about how well you've done. And since you've just completed something that was horrifying to you, it's not surprising that you might think you did a poor job, when actually you did just fine.

Establishing a rapport with your audience, both on stage and off, is therefore a crucial aspect of your public speaking. How else can you hope to gain a true sense of your accomplishments? And as you've already established, it is your experiences with past presentations that will influence you as public speakers now and in the future.

If these descriptions are familiar to you, you may be thinking the whole discussion is somewhat depressing. However, it is important to recognize your personal reactions to the public speaking situation for several reasons. First of all, it's a common misconception that "I'm the only one who experiences ..." For those who tend to get red blotches on their face and neck, you should realize that many people experience red blotches. Those who tend to avoid the situation altogether should realize that avoidance is a common reaction to the fear-inducing stimulus of public speaking. Also, if you find that your thoughts are scattered when you attempt to give a speech, you need to know that many successful public speakers have learned to deal with the same distractions.

And that's the bottom line. It is possible to learn to manage anxiety about speaking. If your hands shake, your knees quiver, you get a dry mouth, or you feel dizzy when you get in front of an audience, take heart. With proper attention to changing a few behaviors, you can get these responses under control.

Good public speakers are usually considered good because they have learned processes by which they can control their fear. Unfortunately, we tend to compare ourselves to what we think a good or bad speaker looks like. And usually, you will decide you look more like a bad speaker than a good one. This is due, in large part, to what you know about public speaking and to your preconceived beliefs and misconceptions.

# Chapter Three

## What We Know and What We Think We Know

**The "Good" Speaker**

Everybody who gives a public speech has some idea as to what makes a good public speaker. Maybe you think of words that have been spoken in the past by famous politicians, such as Ronald Reagan's famous sound bite, "Mr. Gorbachev, tear down this wall!" The authority and confidence with which Reagan delivered his speech, and that line in particular, made all the difference. This speech is now widely considered to be a milestone in the history of the Cold War. Perhaps Reagan was a highly gifted writer. Maybe it was only his experience as an actor that allowed him to play the part of a strong and determined leader. All that is certain is that he portrayed a sense of strength and intelligence while speaking to the public.

It is important to remember that you are not expected to be a "Ronald Reagan" public speaker. In fact, by setting your goals to unrealistic heights, you are inevitably going to disappoint yourself. While your audience may be more than simply satisfied, your own expectations will be diminished. Most of us can look at Martin Luther King Jr., or Maya Angelou, or Lee Iaccoca, and say to ourselves, "I could never be a speaker like that." But then, the negative message in our brain becomes, "I could never be a speaker." If you begin to define a good speaker by the characteristics of a great speaker, then you will find it difficult to ever accept the fact that you might, yourself, be a very effective presenter.

**The "Bad" Speaker**

On the other hand, if you are not careful, and especially if you are not very confident about our skills, you may come to define a bad speaker as a speaker who shares your own characteristics. Actually, it is more likely that you define a bad speaker by the absence of the characteristics which you use to describe a good speaker. For example, you may say that a good speaker is one who speaks confidently. Therefore, a bad speaker is one who is not confident.

Our definitions of good and bad speakers might include statements that seem to be specific when actually they are not. You might say that a good speaker maintains good eye contact. What do you mean by "maintains?" Does that mean a good speaker always looks at the audience? What do you mean by "good eye contact?" Does that mean that a speaker can maintain bad eye contact? If so, how?

What you probably mean is that a good speaker looks at the audience often and looks at various audience members or areas of the audience when speaking to them. But in your mind, it is easy to use the vagueness of "good" and "maintains" in order to prove that you are not a good speaker. By thinking abstractly about what makes good eye contact, it is simple for to imagine that you are not capable of doing it.

That's the case with all of the characteristics you consider to be proof of a good speaker. If you are not entirely sure what you mean, the easiest avenue to take is the one that leads to, "I can't do it." If you're not careful, you will proceed to do everything in your power to prove that you are right, that you can't do it. This is the self-fulfilling prophecy mentioned earlier. Once you have decided that you will fail, it is only natural that your actions will reflect your thoughts: You will act as if you have already failed.

**Performance Orientation Evaluation Orientation**

Part of the reason for this self-fulfilling prophecy is that you orient yourself to regarding the speech as a performance, rather than as a communication event. In so doing, you enact probably the most common and most harmful of the misconceptions about public speaking-that the speech is a performance. By focusing on the performance of a speech, you focus on yourself instead of the message or purpose of the presentation.

The performance approach to public speaking has been taught, and in some cases is still being taught, in many classrooms, seminars, and workshops. The philosophy of this approach is that a good speaker looks, sounds, and acts like a skilled orator. Back in the time of the Greek philosopher Aristotle, an entire rhetorical practice was based on teaching speakers to appear credible, honest, and trustworthy.

This philosophy was, of course, not totally agreed upon by the great thinkers. Many of the great minds of the time felt that it was a speaker's job to speak with the audience, not to enact some performance with grace and flourish. If the speaker were indeed able to perform well and still succeed in persuading his audience, then all the better. But it was the communicative intent, not performance that was seen by many as most important.

From the time of your elementary school book reports and recitations, you have been trained that a speaker "performs" a speech for the audience. This orientation produces a lot of uncomfortable pressures surrounding the public speaking event. By adopting a performance orientation, you put yourself in the spotlight of the event. A performance implies that there will be an audience watching us for the purpose of enjoying our display. You more the actor than the communicator and your focus needs to be on the audience as a third party who needs to be appeased. The actor, for example, knows whether or not he or she has been successful by the applause given from an audience, or the rapt attention focused on the performance. This audience response is a form of approval; it shows a positive evaluation of the player by the audience.

While public speakers enjoy applause, and audiences enjoy applauding good speakers, it is not the evaluation of performance that the speaker should be focused on. Rather, the speaker should think about whether or not he or she was able to effectively communicate the ideas contained within his or her presentation. When you adopt a performance orientation to public speaking, you tend to think of the speech only in terms of how well you will do as an actor. You fantasize about moving gracefully across the stage, with smooth, sweeping gestures that emphasize and illustrate your points. You imagine your voice, strong and confident, sounding a fluent and compelling set of words so that the audience is impressed with both our presence and our delivery.

The fact of the matter is, if you were to ask the audience members after the speech whether or not the speech was successful, most of them would base their answer on whether they understood what the speaker was trying to accomplish and felt that they gained value from the experience.

If you tend to focus on performance, you also tend to focus on your personal evaluation by the audience. The good actor is applauded, with shouts of bravo and congratulations after the performance. The bad actor is booed off the stage and finds that he or she gets little or no support after the performance. Nobody wants the type of negative evaluation that an audience gives to a poor comedian or actor. The pressure of a performance evaluation is intense. Yet it is that sort of pressure you are likely to exert on yourself.

By now you are probably thinking, "Fine. If it's not a performance, then what exactly is a public speech?" A public speech is an opportunity for a speaker to communicate an idea or ideas to a group of people. It is an opportunity to persuade an audience in accordance with the proposed purpose of the speech and the intent of the speaker. That is it. That is all.

A speech defined in that manner is successful under one condition; that the speaker communicates effectively with the audience. Not to the audience. You communicate to an audience when you perform for their observation. A successful speaker involves the audience through compelling content. Delivery is only important inasmuch as it adds to or takes away from the purpose of the speech.

If you allow yourself to think of public speaking as a conversation, rather than as a performance, you will find that you have relieved a great deal of pressure that goes along with being an actor. A good speaker may occasionally stutter, or perhaps have a voice that is a little softer than might be desired. But if that speaker has information that the audience needs to have, or has an opinion that the audience recognizes as compelling enough to consider, then the stuttering, soft-voiced speaker is a more effective public speaker than the slick, smooth, fluent speaker who really has nothing to say.

In fact, audiences are a lot more forgiving than you usually give them credit for being. Think about the last time you were in an audience for a public speech. If the speaker stutters, or has a unique dialect, or perhaps looks more at the podium than at the audience, you do indeed notice it. Briefly. Then, you usually ignore it and focus your attention on what the speaker is saying. You say to yourself, "Oh, she's nervous" or "What an interesting dialect." Then you forget it. If you are there to hear a speaker, your purpose as an audience member is to receive information. You watch a comedian to be entertained, but you listen to a speaker to be informed.

By establishing a realistic expectation of good and bad speakers, and by relieving yourself of the responsibility to perform an Oscar-winning performance, you can begin to establish an atmosphere of control and assurance. These are the prerequisites to speaking with comfort. In order to create an environment of successful communication through public presentation, you will want to create as much predictability as you can.

**Fear of the Unexpected**

What really is going to happen when you give your speech? Is the audience going to rise up in exultant ovation? Are they going to mob the stage when you're finished, attempting to get an autograph or a lock of hair? Are you going to have to get an unlisted number because of all the calls you receive at home to praise you for your outstanding presentation? Or will your audience literally "boo" you off the stage? Will they be so bored that your speech is constantly disrupted by the sound of bodies falling asleep and sliding out of chairs? Will they bring fruits and vegetables to fling on stage during your speech? Or will the host of the event stand up at about the midpoint of your presentation and ask you to please sit down and shut up?

None of these things is actually likely to happen. You will likely not be the greatest speaker that the audience has ever heard, nor will you be the worst. It is unlikely that you are going to put your audience into a state of awe because of your brilliant oratory style and it is unlikely that you will be chased from the building because of your horrible speech. What is most likely is that your presentation will fall squarely in between these extremes. There will be some elements of your speech that you will have done very well. There will be other aspects that could be improved upon. But that's the case with all of our endeavors. It's the rare situation that can't be improved, and it's the rare situation that is the best possible scenario.

You should strive to make the public speaking event as predictable as possible. Consider the realistic outcomes of your presentation. It is unlikely that your audience will react in any extreme way to your speech, but rather will be supportive and want to see you succeed. Through preparation and practice, you will be able to overcome much of the anxiety you face well before actually giving your speech.

Through recognizing that speech anxiety is a common phenomenon, experienced by most speakers to some degree, you should understand that you are not alone in your feelings of nervousness and that this nervousness can be channeled into the excitement necessary for you to produce a good, solid speech. To make that energy a positive force, you need to develop some strategies for dealing with the anxiety that you know you're going to experience. The next chapter will give you some suggestions and methods to consider for changing anxiety to excitement and creating a successful public speaking event.

# Chapter Four

## Nervous Excitement versus Nervous Anxiety

*When I have to give a presentation, I can feel the adrenaline all the way to the ends of my hairs. I start fluttering my fingers and I can't stand still. When I stand at the podium, if I'm not careful, I raise the heels of my feet up and down. Then, when it's over, I continue to be hyper. I swear that I could run the New York Marathon when I'm giving a speech.*

While it may be difficult for this speaker's audience to listen to her presentation while running with her through Manhattan, she feels she has the stamina and excitement "run the New York Marathon" when she's giving a speech. Interestingly enough, if she were to do some form of physical exercise before she gave her speech, she would be engaging in one of the most effective methods to control the nervous feelings she experiences during the presentation.

A brisk walk around the building or a couple of push-ups in the office (honestly!) can help relieve some of the stress because it "fools" the body into using up some of that extra fuel. Remember, the body is gearing itself up for physical engagement. If you undertake some sort of light exercise, your body will rapidly dissipate much of the chemical buildup that occurs when the fight or flight system kicks into action.

Physical action helps relieve anxiety in numerous ways. For one thing, the focus on activity can distract your mind enough to avoid the obsessing that sometimes happens before a speech. That alone is worth something. More importantly, as you exercise lightly, the increase in blood pressure is reduced, the chemicals such as adrenaline are dissipated in your body, and the effect of these chemicals on the brain (and the effect of the chemicals on your body which then affect the brain) is rapidly reduced as well. In other words, exercise helps reduce the physiological effect on the psychological process.

Obviously, it's going to be difficult to tote the stationary bicycle with you to every presentation you make. But you can take a short walk, run in place for a couple of moments, or simply jump up and down a few times. Just remember that you're not really engaging in this exercise to tone up flabby muscles or lose a few extra pounds. The point is to just get the blood circulating a bit; so take it easy. If you get to the point where you're panting for breath, or your clothes are beginning to stick to your body, you're doing too much!

**Relaxation**

If it is possible to do some sort of physical action before your speech you should do it. However, this alone will likely only reduce the sharp edge that anxiety brings with the body's reaction to stress. Along with some form of physical movement, relaxation techniques can go a long way in providing you with the confidence and focus to be a strong presenter.

Exercise and relaxation are not the opposite activities that they appear to be at first glance. This makes relaxation a valuable complement to exercise. While there are some relaxation exercises that require a lot of time and a lot of room, you can usually develop the skill to relax with just a few moments and with no special space requirements.

As stated earlier, the fight or flight response activates the sympathetic part of the autonomic nervous system, resulting in bodily activity that contributes to the feeling of anxiety and lack of control. The relaxation response, on the other hand, activates the parasympathetic part of the autonomic nervous system, resulting in such effects as slowed heart rate, increased salivation and digestion, and lowered blood pressure. In other words, the parasympathetic system is designed to offset the effects of the sympathetic system, the part that is causing you the most problem with speech anxiety.

There are literally hundreds of relaxation methods that have been proven effective for some people at some time, including meditation, self-hypnosis, visualization, and so on. If you already have a favorite method, or discover one that works better for you, that's great. Use it. You may even find that you're able to develop your own method of inducing the relaxation response. For most individuals, the most effective technique is a matter of personal preference, that is, the one with which the individual is most comfortable. While there are two techniques covered here, make sure to find one that fits you.

It is really nothing more than a commonsense observation that one must be comfortable with a chosen relaxation technique in order for it to be of any benefit. In many Eastern traditions, for example, it is considered necessary for the one who is relaxing to lose the sense of his or her own body. That is, one must be so comfortable as to gain an intense inward focus. It seems logical then that practices such as yoga would encourage the use of mats and other devices to help one forget about the body.

With whatever method that is chosen, some people find it easier to begin practicing their relaxation exercise with the help of a pre-recorded audio guide. You may discover that, as your body relaxes, your mind tends to relax as well, sometimes making it difficult to concentrate on remembering what you are supposed to do next. There are many of these tapes on the market.

**Active Relaxation**

Although it at first sounds like a contradiction in terms, Active Relaxation can be an effective method of relaxing before a speech or anytime you feel tense. The principle at work behind Active Relaxation is one of "opposite and equal reaction." Simply put, when you take an already tense muscle, contract it even further, and then relax the muscle, the muscle will return to a state more relaxed than when it started.

You can test this method right now while reading this book. Take a moment to become aware of your right upper arm. This can be done to any muscle group, but we'll say the right upper arm just for the sake of the example.

Notice the tension that exists right now in your biceps. If you're holding the book with your right hand, you'll notice there are some muscles that are tensed in order to keep the book upright. Unless you are a very relaxed person and you haven't even gotten up from bed yet, your muscle probably has some tension whether or not you are holding the book with your right hand.

Once you think you have a fair idea of how your biceps feels right now, start to tense the muscle through contraction. Tense it as tight as you can without going into a muscle cramp. If you're still holding the book with your right hand, you're probably finding that it's getting hard to read because your arm is shaking! Put the book in your other hand or lay it down where you can continue reading.

Hold the tension for a count of two. Now, relax the muscle as totally and completely as you can. Lay your forearm on your leg or on the table so you don't have to use your biceps to keep your arm elevated. Notice the tension in your biceps now. Most people will discover that the muscle is less tense now than when they started. If you can't tell a difference (or even if you can), do the exercise one more time. If you limit yourself to no more than about three times doing the exercise, you should find that each time brings about more relaxation in the muscle.

Now, imagine this exercise for your entire body. You need to stretch out on a bed or the floor, or at least sit in a comfortable chair. Starting with your forehead, work your way down your body, one muscle group at a time, tensing and then relaxing. The first time you do this, it may take as much as twenty minutes to make it all the way through the body. With practice and experience, you'll be able to move a bit faster.

While this is an effective way to relax, there are a couple of problem areas for most people. For one thing, it's easy for us to tense and relax our biceps. It's something you do all the time and you don't look particularly weird when you do it. But tensing up our face is another matter. To tense the muscles in your face you have to furrow your eyebrows, squinch up your nose, pout your lips, and wrinkle your chin.

Except for one case mentioned a couple of years ago in one of the supermarket tabloids, nobody I'm aware of has ever had their face freeze in that position. But there is something encoded in our brain that makes screwing up our face like that almost laughable even if we're by ourselves with no chance of being seen by somebody else. So, if you have trouble with this part, first make sure you are someplace where you are unlikely to be seen. Second, if it strikes you as funny, then laugh. Nothing can be as relaxing as a good laugh anyway.

Another problem that can occur lies in trying to tense the muscles too much. You should tense the muscle as much as is comfortable to hold for three to four seconds. If the muscle starts to cramp at all, you are tensing too hard. This may simply mean that you should try again without contracting the muscle group quite so much. Or, you may want to go on to a different method of relaxation.

A similar problem is that there are some individuals who may have physical challenges that make Active Relaxation inappropriate. If that's the case, remember that there are lots of different methods of relaxation. So find one that fits your specific situation.

The final concern with Active Relaxation is that, even if you become an expert, you are almost always going to have to find an area where you can be undisturbed for at least ten minutes. This can be a problem if you're at the local Holiday Inn and preparing to give an after-dinner speech to some civic organization or if you're at a business meeting and are given an hour's notice before having to speak.

Because life is unpredictable, and because part of your goal as a speaker is to make the context of your presentation as predictable as possible, it is important for you to learn more than one relaxation technique. Visualization is an alternative technique that, with practice, requires very little time and little or no isolation. It is also effective for people with physical restrictions when Active Relaxation is inappropriate.

**Visualization**

A lot has been said and written about Visualization in the last few years. In every arena from education to business, authors have touted Visualization as the solution to slow learning, self-defeating practices, and business failure, just to name a few. As a result, the term "Visualization" has come to represent several different concepts and approaches to taking control of your mind.

Like Active Relaxation, your initial attempts at Visualization Relaxation will require a quiet area where you are unlikely to be disturbed for a short period of time. Initially, twenty minutes should be adequate. Many people have discovered that as they gain experience with this technique, they need no more than two to three minutes to achieve relaxation, which of course makes this technique applicable in more public speaking situations.

You should not expect to be the ideal public speaker during your initial public presentations. Nor should you expect to go from twenty minutes to two minutes after practicing Visualization for only a short period. Most things in life require time to learn and perfect. Allow yourself time to acclimate to the Visualization technique by trying it over a period of a few days.

If this is the first time you've ever attempted a Visualization exercise, take a moment to go look at yourself in a mirror. Full-length is preferred. Notice what you're wearing, the color of your clothes, the style of your hair. Turn sideways and get a look at your profile. Turn your back to the mirror and look over your shoulder. In other words, take a moment to see what you look like. This is an interesting exercise in-and-of itself, since most of us see ourselves a lot less than other people see us!

Now, lie down on the floor, in bed, or sit in a comfortable chair. By the way, you're going to have to read through this whole section before you do this exercise because the next direction calls for closing your eyes! Your first goal is to visualize what you probably look like right now, in your chair or on your bed, from about six feet away. Play with this image a little. Imagine what you look like from just a foot or so away. Then imagine pulling back to twelve or fifteen feet. The imagery in your head should be like watching a video that somebody made while you were resting, zooming in close, and then zooming back.

Now, for the sake of discussion, let's say that you are in your bedroom lying on your bed. If you're actually sitting in an easy chair, that's fine too. Just change the appropriate visual images as you read through this. Feel the sensation of your body on the bed. Notice the feel of the sheet or blanket on which you are lying. Notice the pillow under your head and the feel of your heels on the mattress. Try to become as familiar as possible with the things you touch.

Now, visualizing yourself from a few feet away again, slowly watch as the bed turns into a large, white, cotton cloud. Initially, you should do this very slowly, with the bed gradually fading into the round, soft shape of a cloud. With practice, you'll find that you go to this part almost immediately. But for now, enjoy playing with the image again. Start at the top and work your way to the foot of the bed, changing the mattress into a fluffy cloud foot by foot.

Once you can imagine what you would look like lying on a cloud rather than a mattress (or sitting in a chair), try to imagine what lying on a cloud would feel like. It would probably feel something like being suspended in air. Perhaps your cloud is warm. You may want it to be cool. Regardless, it is soft and very comfortable. Imagine how your head would feel on a cloud like this, and your body. Imagine now your heels resting on a cloud rather than some hard surface.

Remember our discussions about Eastern traditions and how some of them encourage that you go into your own mind? You may have noticed that Visualization does much the same thing. By imagining yourself in a soft and comfortable environment, you are working to achieve a feeling of balance and oneness with yourself. Hopefully a sense of calm is enveloping you as you imagine lying on your cloud.

Once you've achieved this image, enjoy it. Nothing should happen rapidly for a few moments. As opposed to what many will tell you, you should not try to force your mind to be void of any other thoughts. Lots of thoughts will come to you – let them. But slow them down. Imagine that your thoughts are all trying to speak at once and you're making them hold up their little hands to take turns. Check your breathing. It should be slow and relaxed.

Now, before you come out of this comfortable situation, you should do a quick assessment of the feeling of relaxation that you are experiencing. Your goal in this assessment is to become familiar enough with how you're feeling so as to be able to recognize the feeling the next time you achieve it. Notice your slow breathing, the feeling of your relaxed muscles, the slow thought-processing you're doing. Notice how calm you can be.

When you're ready, imagine that your cloud is once again slowly changing into a bed (or chair or whatever). Don't be in a hurry, but as gradually as it changed into a cloud, the image in your brain should change into a bed. Imagine yourself lying on the bed again for a moment or two, and then open your eyes. With more practice, this peaceful feeling can follow you onto center stage as you encounter your audience and as you make your presentation.

Neat, huh? Our mind is an amazing thing. You have an incredible ability to recall not only spoken messages, but visual, tactile, and olfactory (smell) messages as well. You can remember the exact sensations of how an object felt, or how something smelled. Visualization allows us to put this ability to work. You, of course, were never really lying on a cloud, nor have you ever. But you have felt soft sheets before, or the soft coolness of a breeze. When you try to imagine something you've never experienced, your brain will go through all the "sense memories" available to try to come up with what would be the closest sensation.

What you will have actually experienced after practicing Visualization is a type of self-hypnosis. Hypnosis is simply a jousting of the mind. You will have chosen to focus on something pleasant. But the real goal in this exercise lies in the final moments. Each time you do this, you want to try to reinforce the memory of your relaxed state as if you were in control of your thoughts and lying on that cloud.

While the brain is good at storing information about events that have actually happened, the mind will also store information about events that you have imagined. As a result, you will find that recalling that relaxed state becomes easier as you become more experienced at using this exercise. In fact, after just two or three times going through the entire scenario, you'll find that as soon as you close your eyes you can imagine that you are lying on the cloud. Then, you'll find that you are able to simply "recall" the feeling of total relaxation and may not even need to imagine yourself doing anything at all. Believe it or not, with just a little practice you'll be able to recall the relaxed state without even closing your eyes. The trick is in being able to focus your mind, and like most of our other endeavors, practice makes it easier.

As with Active Relaxation, there are a couple of common problem areas you should think about. First of all, the most common problem with the Visualization exercise is that you may actually fall asleep. If you are going to use this technique to calm down before giving a speech, I also urge you not to use this technique to help you sleep at night in the beginning. Once you are able to bring about your relaxed state without going through the whole visualization process, and then by all means use it if you need to relax yourself before going to sleep. But don't train yourself to go to sleep during the Visualization protocol. The best bet in learning to do this is to try to make sure you are already rested (sleep wise) before attempting the exercise.

The second problem is that Visualization is focused mind activity. As a result, when you are focusing on the visualization, you are not going to be able to focus on much else. This is not an appropriate activity to do while driving, operating machinery, or doing anything else that requires your attention. Once you've learned to relax on demand, you may find that relaxing is anything but distracting. But initially, don't practice this exercise when you need to concentrate on anything else.

Some people find that their initial attempts at this exercise are difficult because they have to remember "what comes next." This is a common problem that has a couple of solutions. You can record a tape or have someone record it for you. If you choose the second method, you should write a script that moves you slowly through the relaxation and visualization and then practice it several times before recording. There's nothing particularly compelling about the monotone of somebody reading a script, or stumbling over a particular phrase.

The second method is to purchase a tape with a visualization method professionally recorded on it. These tapes usually have a soothing background and have been edited so that the timing is correct and mistakes have been taken out.

**Combinations**

Many people find that they are able to combine relaxation approaches for an extremely effective personal relaxation method. For example, you might use Active Relaxation to achieve initial physical comfort and then Visualization Relaxation to calm your mind. Or you might use Visualization Relaxation to achieve calmness and then other relaxation methods to achieve further goals you may have.

Any combination that works for you is a good combination. You may even be able to visualize yourself doing Active Relaxation (honestly!). There are no wrong combinations. As long as you are able to find, and become familiar with, the relaxation response, you will be able to increase your ability to relax in stressful situations.

And as this ability increases, you will find that preparing a speech becomes a much less nerve-wracking endeavor.

If you use a combination of relaxation techniques, you may observe that you are able to be more creative in your presentations. Part of this is a natural outgrowth of being relaxed. But it is also happening because you have been exercising your creativity as well as your muscles and your brain.

**Controlled Substances**

As a final word in this chapter, a couple of things should be said about using controlled substances. Many people attempt to "self-medicate" public speaking anxiety by having a few drinks before giving a speech or taking a sedative (or even smoking a joint). Without trying to sound too preachy, I have to say that this is a bad idea for several reasons.

First, the body's ability to overwhelm foreign substances should not be underestimated. For example, while alcohol has the ability to lower inhibitions and slow down the central nervous system, the body has an equal, and sometimes more powerful, ability to speed things up. So the tendency to overindulge becomes a real temptation. While one cocktail may calm some people after a particularly stressful day at work, it will probably take more than that to calm the type of anxiety many feel before they give a speech. As a result, the speaker will have two or three or more drinks before the speech. Then, rather than being calm, he or she is intoxicated.

And, commonly, more worried about the speech than before. You may think you can't give a speech, but if you're drunk, you really do have something to worry about.

The other problem with using controlled substances is that our judgment inevitably becomes impaired. You imagine things are going better (or worse) when actually they are not. Our thought processes become scattered and it becomes even more difficult to concentrate than before. An impaired lack of mental ability is not exactly what you want to display when you give a public presentation.

The final thing to remember is that there is not a chemical depressant in existence that only calms the nerves. The more effective the substance is to calm us psychologically, the more likely it is to slow us down physically as well. This means that movements become over-exaggerated because you attempt to compensate for the slowness. You lift your feet less high and as a result are more likely to stumble. Most noticeable is the tendency to slur consonants when you are under the influence of a depressant.

All of these physical symptoms of controlled-substance abuse can make the public speaking situation many times worse than it would be otherwise. The main problem with using controlled substances is that the more you use the less in control you are. And remember, our goal is to make an unpredictable situation predictable. This is an impossible achievement if you have made yourself unpredictable by using some sort of drug to calm down. So as our past First Lady Nancy Reagan said, "Just Say No!"

**Summary**

Turning nervous anxiety into nervous excitement can be a challenge. But it can be done. Take the time to get to know your anxiety, how it feels, what the symptoms are, and when it starts. Then create a plan to deal with it. The cycle of nervous anxiety looks something like this: Mental anxiety leads to physical tension which leads to more mental anxiety which leads to more physical tension and on and on. You can break this cycle at any point: By calming your mind you'll calm your body.

By calming your body, you will calm your mind. It takes practice, but probably not as much practice as you think. Making a concerted effort to get your brain and body under control can give amazing results in a short period of time. And when you see these results, you'll be better able to enjoy the excitement of giving a presentation rather than simply experiencing the anxiety of public speaking.

Of course, getting your initial fears out of the way is a big step in putting together a successful presentation, but it is only one step. Once you've begun to put into practice some of the exercises outlined in this chapter, you'll be better prepared to focus on the creation and delivery of your message. And isn't that what you're giving a speech for anyway?

# Chapter Five

## Presenting the Speech

The actual process of gathering information and formulating your presentation is outside of the scope of this specific text. In fact, to become a truly great public speaker, you should read the books and listen to some of the great tapes that are in the marketplace as well regarding the construction of your message. If you would like some suggestions or advice, please feel free to send a note to info@impactsuccess.com and tell us what you are looking for. We would be glad to give you recommendations.

There are still some basic approaches and principles that should be followed in the creation and presentation of your speech. You will find if you read or listen to other material on the topic, these principles will be core to most of the successful methods of developing presentation messages that are available.

Regardless of message, there are some basic questions you need to answer prior to the actual presentation of the speech. From a topic standpoint, what will be the purpose and subject of your speech? While subject should be obvious, purpose is the answer to the question, "What do you want your audience to do as a result of your presentation?"

Many publications, including some prior publications of this author, give various presentation objectives including a "Speech to inform." While this makes sense at some level if you are thinking of presenting to people in order for them to learn something, it is not a very helpful designation. Regardless of topic and audience, you are presenting in order for them to actually do something.

It might be that what you want them to do is to physically take action. Perhaps you want them to believe something differently than they already do. That is an action on the audience's part. The "Speech to inform" has the problem of not answering the question "Why?" Presentations filled with information should still have an objective at the end for audience members to make a change. Perhaps the change is in their appreciation for the material or in their application of the material. But if there is nothing asked of the audience as a part of your presentation, it will stand to be boring and one-sided.

The bottom line: Think about "What do I want my audience to do as a result of listening to me?"

Second, figure out exactly who your audience is going to be. Determine approximately how many people will be in the audience. Are they your age? If not, what might you have in common with them in relation to the subject of your speech? Why are they there? If they are compelled to attend for some reason, then you want to make sure that they get enough value from your presentation that they see their time as well spent. If they volunteered to be there, it is likely that they have an interest in your topic to begin with. If they paid to be there, then they truly have an interest!

Third, determine the best way of presenting to your audience. Would a computer-generated slideshow be the most helpful? Perhaps something a bit lower-tech like a flip chart (several large pieces of paper on an easel). Would your audience get value from seeing objects or models related to your topic?

Something that is critical to consider here is the concept of place. It would be a waste of time for you to create a flip chart for use in a large auditorium. Similarly, you would not want to create a slideshow if there is not a screen on which to show it. It is important to know what space you will be using for your speech before you show up to give it. In fact, if you know what the space will be well ahead of time, the image of this space can aid in your visualization!

The fourth aspect to consider is time. How long does your audience expect your presentation to be? For most people, twenty to forty-five minutes is a normal expectation. If it is much beyond that you are not talking about a single speech as much as you might be looking at a workshop or series of presentations.

Many speakers who are passionate about their topic will minimize the issue of time because they feel they should use however much is necessary in order to be successful in their presentation. While it is laudable that you feel strongly about your topic, it is also important to remember that your audience members have valuable time invested as well. Being given 30 minutes to speak and taking an hour is not only less effective, it indicates to your audience (and possibly your host) that you consider your priorities and your time to take precedent over theirs. Make sure to know how much time you have available and then construct your speech to accommodate that time.

Finally, be prepared to answer questions from the audience. This may happen as part of your presentation, or as an aside with interested members of the group after you have finished. Make sure to do enough extra research to have answers to common questions. Also be able to recommend sources of additional information... just in case you encounter a question that you are unable to answer.

The only other thing to really say in the scope of this book about the writing of your speech is: Don't forget the earlier discussion about procrastination. The only way you will feel comfortable giving a speech is if you are prepared far enough in advance to have plenty of time practicing and becoming familiar with what you have to say. Last-minute preparation is a nightmare for even the most confident and experienced speaker, so start putting your speech together early.

What you will concern ourselves most with here is the actual delivery of the speech. Although you probably worry about delivery from the moment you know you are going to give a speech, the delivery of your speech is the final element of giving a presentation. While you sometimes get obsessed with how well you speak, the fact of the matter is that audiences pay less attention to a speaker's delivery than they do to the speaker's message. If a speaker is too quiet, or speaks too fast, audience members will typically acknowledge this to themselves, thinking "Wow, she speaks softly," and then proceed to listen to what the speaker has to say. In other words, as the speaker, you tend to think more about delivery than does your audience.

That is not to say that delivery isn't important. Delivery is important inasmuch as it adds to or takes away from the effectiveness of your speech. Delivery is an important element, but only one element in the public speaking situation. And there are several things you can do to make sure your delivery is as helpful to your goals as possible.

**Delivery**

Your decision about the types of notes you are going to use to give your speech will greatly affect your presentation. Please make note that the following recommendations do not apply to professional speakers. Those who chose to make a living at speaking have to "raise the bar" a bit and be able to present their topic without the aid of notes. Most of you reading this book will not be trying to become professional speakers so you don't need to worry about this too much. If you are either a professional speaker or want to take your delivery to that level, there are some great training programs out there that can give you guidance. The internationally acclaimed motivational speaker, Les Brown, does an outstanding training that you can investigate by visiting his site, www.lesbrown.com.

While many people successfully put speaker's notes together on 8.5 x 11 inch paper, I recommend using simple index cards. They are cheap, easy to handle, and will help you avoid writing too much information to use in presenting your speech. Also, if your hand does shake a little, it is a lot harder for the observer to notice when you are holding note cards than when you are holding a full sheet of paper. Note cards are developed from the outline of your speech by using the key words found in the main points, subordinate points, and supporting material. The note cards should contain only enough information to remind you of what you want to say and the order in which you should say it. Only in the case of complicated statistics or direct testimony requiring exact wording should you use word-for-word phrasing on your note cards.

Note cards are an excellent aid to remembering the content and structure of your speech while still allowing you the freedom to adapt to your audience on the spur of the moment. Here are some tips about using note cards:

1. Use only key words on your note cards, never complete sentences. If you write your speech out word

for word on your cards, you will almost always be tempted to read it to your audience.

2. Limit the number of cards you use. The fewer you have, the freer you are to interact with your audience. One good rule of thumb is to use one card for your introduction, one card for each main point and one card for your conclusion.

3. Use 3 x 5 or 4 x 6 cards, not slips of paper. Paper is sloppy and unpredictable, whereas cards are easier to handle and look uniform.

4. Always number your cards. This tip can save you a great deal of embarrassment if you drop your cards on your way to give the speech.

5. Although typewritten is OK, there is no reason why you shouldn't handwrite your note cards, as long as you can read them. Cutting up your outline and pasting it onto note cards defeats the purpose of using notes and will make you sound as if you're reading your speech.

6. Remember that the note cards are for you. Use your own system of symbols, abbreviations, little drawings, whatever will help. As long as you know what they mean, they are acceptable.

7. The only way to successfully give a public presentation, and the only way to successfully use note cards, is to be prepared at least a day or so in advance and practice, practice, practice.

Why not write your speech out word-for-word, or memorize your speech?

For one thing, the spoken word is noticeably different than the written word. When you make a complete manuscript of your speech, and then read it to the audience, it usually sounds exactly like somebody reading a manuscript. Boring! It is difficult to concentrate on your audience and your content when you are busy reading word for word from your paper. The normal reaction to a manuscript speech is, "If you wanted me to read it, why didn't you just give me a copy?"

There are occasions where a manuscript speech is appropriate, but these occasions are rare. If you are speaking on a matter that is of such importance that each word must be chosen accurately with no room for error, then a manuscript may be what you need. For example, the president of the United States uses manuscripts when giving a speech because his words form policy. A company spokesperson may use a manuscript to issue a statement of policy because the spoken word could result in litigation. So it would be important for each word to be exactly spoken as written.

Most of your speeches will probably not fall into these categories, so a manuscript speech is not the way to go for you. Reading a script is difficult, not only because it is hard to sound enthusiastic, but because it is easy for you to lose your place or stumble over specific words and phrases. The written word tends to have longer sentences and more difficult words to pronounce than the spoken word, so using a manuscript doesn't ease your burden, it increases it.

A memorized speech at least has the advantage of allowing more audience eye contact than a manuscript speech. But for most people, a memorized speech sounds very much like a manuscript speech. To actually memorize a speech word for word requires enormous effort. For an average, one page of double-spaced text equals one minute of speech. That would be twenty pages you would need to memorize to give a twenty minute speech.

Memorization also increases anxiety dramatically. It is easy to see why: If you have memorized your speech, you will be more worried about remembering each word and sentence than about whether or not your audience understands your message. Memorization makes us concentrate on specific words rather than specific thoughts. This will also detract from an otherwise successful speech.

So the route you need to go, and that you need to practice, is speaking with the use of speaker's notes. By the way, this is called extemporaneous speaking, and is the preferred method for nervous speakers. Extemporaneous speeches allow the speaker to make eye contact with the audience and to sound more enthusiastic about the speech.

These speeches are more like conversations. If you recall from earlier in the book, this is the exact perception you should have of your speech: a conversation with your audience. With practice, you will find speaking with notes to be the easiest method of giving a public speech. But it takes quite a bit of practice. Since you've prepared for your speech ahead of time, however, you now have the leisure of having the time you need to adequately prepare the delivery of your presentation.

The first step is to take the outline you drafted for your speech and use it as a script. Practice alone the first few times, stumbling your way through the speech until you are pretty familiar with the introduction, the progression of the content of your speech, and the conclusion. Then make the speaker's notes as outlined earlier.

Now, with your outline handy, attempt to give the speech using your speaker's notes. Be careful not to write too much on your note cards because the more you write, the more like a manuscript speech your presentation becomes. And trust me; if the script is in front of you when you start to give your speech, you will read it. So practice a few times with just the note cards.

If you get stuck, pick up the outline and get going again. Your goal is to get all the way through using just the note cards at first. Then, after a couple of times through the speech, you'll find that you are able to make your presentation while just referring to your notes occasionally in order to stay on track. By pulling yourself away from a total dependence on your notes, you'll be able to improve the other elements of your delivery, such as volume, rate, enthusiasm, and eye contact.

There are some simple rules about these other delivery elements that you should consider once you've practiced your speech a few times. Don't worry about these things initially; wait until you're somewhat familiar with your speech. Then you can start putting the icing on the cake!

**Volume**

In most cases, the nervous public speaker will speak softer than is desirable while giving a presentation. This reflects our lack of confidence in ourselves and essentially gives the impression that you don't really want to be heard. So speak louder than you think you should. To you it might sound as if you're practically yelling. But to your audience, the natural tendency to be softer will be offset by the attempt to be louder. The end result is usually a volume that is clear and understandable to the audience members. If you are one of the rare individuals who actually speak too loudly when you are nervous, or if you are faced with a sensitive microphone, then you should practice in front of a friend and get some feedback about your volume before you give your presentation.

**Rate**

Nervous speakers have a tendency to speak faster than they should when giving a presentation. There seems to be a rush to getting the words out, perhaps because the faster you speak, the faster the presentation will be over. This is what I call "The horse smells the barn" phenomenon. If you've ever been a horse rider, you may have experienced the situation where the horse catches a glimpse of the stall while you are out riding. Many times, before you know it, you find yourself back in the stall where you started. Speaking too quickly can become a major issue, especially if you are a student. Many teachers may like to give you time requirements, "Your speech should last at least ten minutes," for example. Project grades are oftentimes heavily influenced by your adherence to these required time limits.

So the obvious solution to this problem is to speak slower than you think you should. As with the suggestion concerning volume, your natural tendency to speak rapidly will be offset by your attempt to speak slowly. As a result, your enunciation will be improved and your audience will be able to take the time to listen and absorb what you have to say.

Volume and rate are the two primary elements of vocal delivery that affect a speaker's ability to be understood. The combination of these elements affects your overall clarity as well. For example, if you are giving a speech and speak with a single volume and at a consistent rate, you are speaking in what is normally called a monotone. Varying the volume and rate of your speech is an effective way to avoid this problem and to keep your audience engaged in your speech. Think about a conversation with a friend. Sometimes you speak fast, sometimes slow. Sometimes you almost whisper and other times you almost yell. If you think of your speech as a conversation, it is likely that the variation in your speaking voice will improve.

Also, if you are concerned about an international or even regional accent to your voice, you should not become overly obsessed with clarity. Simply by speaking loudly and slowly, most of your audience members will be able to understand you quite well. It doesn't matter if you are from southeast Boston or Pakistan. The reason your audience can't understand you is because the words seem to flow together, and if you are soft-spoken the problem is exaggerated.

If, on the other hand, you are from the Deep South, then you might want to pick up the pace a little. But not much. The problem is still that it is hard for the unfamiliar ear to tell when one word ends and the next word begins. Speaking loudly and slowly will increase your ability to enunciate and your audience's ability to understand.

**Eye Contact**

Eye contact is another important element of public speaking. Although empirical research has yet to confirm the truth in this, you still believe that an honest person looks us in the eye. To build credibility, you should attempt to make eye contact as much and with as many people as possible. If you don't look at your audience, you can't know if they understand your message, or if they perhaps have questions they would like to ask.

There is also a kind of "dirty trick" that is related to eye contact. If we, as audience members, notice the speaker looking at us, then we feel overwhelmingly compelled to look at the speaker. It's a trick that school teachers have known for ages! So one way to keep your audience's attention is to make sure that you look at them. As a result, they will keep their eyes, and their minds, focused on what you have to say.

If you have trouble making eye contact with your audience, then begin by making eye contact with one member of your audience. Do not look over the heads of your audience. Unless you are speaking to several hundred people, the individuals listening to your speech will experience an urge to turn around to see what you are looking at. So make eye contact with one person. Then, as you become a little more comfortable, find somebody else to look at as well. Look back and forth occasionally from the one person to the other. If you do this fairly slowly you will actually appear to be making eye contact with several people. And, in fact, you probably will. You will also discover that most eye contact elicits smiles or head nods or other positive feedback. As you receive this feedback, your confidence will become steadier and you will notice that eye contact in general increases your comfort in giving a speech.

**Movement and Gestures**

There are only a couple of things necessary to say about movements and gestures. First, when you feel like moving, move. Second, when you feel like gesturing, gesture.

Actually, it's not quite that easy, but almost. You should attempt to step away from the lectern occasionally just to add some variation to your presentation. Sometimes the situation will keep you from doing this. For example, stepping away from the podium may mean that you are also stepping away from the microphone or out of the light or even off the platform!

Gestures in public speeches should be as natural as gestures in conversation. If you avoid sticking your hands in your pockets, or gripping the lectern as if you are under attack, you'll find that your natural tendency is to occasionally gesture with one or both hands. This is fine. In fact, it is perfect. You are used to seeing occasional gestures and, as you become more comfortable in speaking; your gestures will become more natural and relaxed. And, if you recall the discussion earlier about the stored energy your body has at that moment, you can see that gesturing is a way to help us let off a little of that energy.

One thing to remember is that gestures below the chest are rarely seen by your audience members. Try holding your elbows away from your body a couple of inches. By doing this you will actually raise most of your gestures to almost shoulder height or above. Your audience will then see the gesture and feel the emphasis that is implicated by some sort of hand or arm movement along with your speech.

While some gesturing during your speech is a great addition to your presentation, too much of a good thing can turn bad very rapidly. Do not fall into the "podium-pounding" routine or simply yelling for the purpose of emphasis. Better to let the substance of your presentation speak for itself. When in doubt, have someone you trust observe you as you practice your speech and then ask them for feedback.

**Summary**

Believe it or not, that's all there is to say about delivery. If you remember only one thing about delivery, remember that you are more concerned than the audience is. If you truly give your speeches from an audience-centered approach, focusing on the audience when you speak, rather than on yourself, then it stands to reason that it is the audience's concerns that should be primary in your mind. If you will allow yourself to go with what feels natural, in most cases your volume will be adequate, your rate understandable, your eye contact plentiful and your gestures natural. Don't spend a lot of time worrying about how these elements of delivery should be. It doesn't really matter, as long as your audience can understand you without being too overly distracted.

This brings me to a final word about practice. You really must practice your speech several times before making your presentation. And the last couple of times should be in front of a trusted friend. Try to have your friend sit in front of you at about the distance of the second or third row of audience members. If you find that making eye contact with your friend is distracting, and it may well be since he or she is the only audience member for your practice, then don't make eye contact. But do go through the motions of making eye contact with other imaginary audience members around the room.

And make sure your friend knows that you want honest feedback about your speech, not just about your delivery. Ask your friend if she or he understood what you really wanted to say, or were convinced about your opinion. Tell your friend ahead of time to pay attention to your main points and the flow from one idea to the next. In other words, give your friend some guidelines for critique. You can certainly remind your friend that you are nervous and would appreciate any criticism being given in a sensitive manner. But there is no substitute for getting the feedback of a trusted ally before you give your speech.

# Chapter Six

## The Final Word

The day of the speech has arrived. This time you spent a lot of constructive time in preparation for this speech. You prepared early and focused your speech at your audience. You've practiced your speech time and again and are armed with your index cards with key words and phrases, because you don't need to read a script word for word to your audience. You've gotten the feedback you needed from a friend and adjusted a point here and there to make the speech clear to the audience that you know so well. This is going to be a different experience than you're used to because this time you will have a successful public speaking experience. And all you need is one good experience upon which to build so that each successive speaking experience is more successful than the one before.

Now let's be realistic. Is your speech going to be perfect? Probably not.

There will be points that could have been clearer, phrases that could have been enunciated better, and sections of the speech where your eye contact could have been improved upon. But that's the case with everybody, not just you. It is vitally important that you realize you are only human and are going to make mistakes. But these mistakes will be ten times more noticeable to you than to anybody else in the room.

So make your goals realistic. If you have not been able to make eye contact with anybody when you give a speech, then decide that this time you will make eye contact with three people, three times during your speech. If you have always spoken too quickly, then promise yourself that this time you will speak more slowly during the introduction and the conclusion. "Baby Steps..." You have the tools now to prepare both mentally and technically for giving this presentation. You can do it.

To increase your odds even more, there are a few simple things you can do the day of the speech. First of all, go to bed early the night before. Get rest. Avoid alcohol and, if possible, caffeine. Both of these substances affect the nervous system, which certainly doesn't need any more agitation than it's getting already. Both substances are also diuretics. This means that you will have to urinate more often, which is something else you don't need in the middle of your speech!

Get to the room where you are going to give your presentation early enough that you can walk around a little before people arrive. Sit in the audience area for a moment and view the stage. Visualize yourself giving a good speech. For most people who are apprehensive about public speaking, the images you have of yourself giving a speech are negative. You imagine that you forget the speech (you won't – you have notes) or that you will not make sense (you will - you prepared for this speech) or that you have completely missed the mark and our audience will hate the speech (they won't - you got feedback).

This time, imagine yourself giving a speech that is interesting and engaging. If you are still sitting in an audience chair, imagine that you are actually an audience member at your own speech. And that you are enjoying it! Don't try to make the image in your mind of the greatest speaker of all time. Just imagine that you are an improved speaker. And above all else, smile! If you really want to trick your mind into believing that you're enjoying yourself, smiling will do it every time. It's hard to smile and be mad, and it's hard to smile and be overly nervous.

Speaking of being nervous, don't forget the discussion of nervous excitement versus nervous anxiety. Remember that it is good to be nervous before you give a speech. In fact, it is normal. Decide that the nervousness you feel is actually excitement and that you can and do have it under control.

If you have the opportunity, go somewhere quiet and relax a few moments before the speech. If you're going to be sitting at the head table or on the dais for a while before you actually speak, then get away from the crowd before you have to join the table. Just for a couple of minutes, breathe deeply and slowly and tell yourself that this is going to be a positive experience. Whatever nervous symptom you've experienced in the past will probably come back in some form, but it won't be nearly as distracting this time as it has been in the past.

Then, a few moments before you actually begin your presentation, try to recall the relaxation response that you've been working on. If it doesn't come to you immediately, don't panic. It's working, even you're not initially aware of it. One person with whom I've worked in the past said that she could never get the relaxation response to kick in before she gave a speech. But she could imagine that it had kicked in, and therefore she was able to relax more!

While you are giving your speech, try as hard as possible to concentrate on what you're saying, not necessarily how you're saying it. This is why suggestions like "Imagine your audience naked" and the like are ridiculous for most people. For one thing, it is difficult to conjure up such an image (and you probably don't want to even if you can). More importantly, suggestions like that draw your attention away from the important element of public speaking what you have to say. If you find that you are getting lost, then look more at your notes. But if you can, look at your audience. They are usually quite friendly people who are as supportive as they can be. Remember that the majority of people in the audience wouldn't volunteer to give a public speech either. They are almost always on your side.

When your speech is over, avoid the tendency to over-critique yourself. Remember, you expected to make a few mistakes. Recall them, note them, and decide that you will improve on those mistakes next time. More importantly, look for the areas of your speech in which you did well. Did your audience understand what you had to say? Did they leave your speech at least considering your point of view? Did you give them knowledge they did not previously have? If you can answer yes to any of these questions, or at least guess that you successfully accomplished some of these goals, then your speech was a success. Give yourself your proper due. Pat yourself on the back for the improvements you made. And look for the next opportunity that arises for you to give a public speech. Each time will become easier and soon you'll discover that the anxiety that has made you miserable in the past can become energy that is exciting and enjoyable when you make a public presentation.

---

**Dr. Todd Thomas** is an internationally recognized speaker, author, workshop leader and coach who has worked with over 3000 leaders in over 20 countries. He is the founder of IMPACT Consulting and Development, LLC (www.impactsuccess.com) and has been interviewed on Fox News, Fox Business, and CNBC. Dr. Todd is also a weekly columnist on *"Leadership Matters"* for TheStreet.com. He is the author of *"Leading in a Flat World: How Good Leaders become Greatly Valued"* and *"Life Lessons for Leaders."*

If you are interested in finding out more about Todd or IMPACT consulting, please visit www.drtoddthomas.com.